88 GOD GIVEN Poems for ENCOURAGEMENT

88 GOD GIVEN *Poems for* ENCOURAGEMENT

MISS JERRY LEE SCHOCK

88 God Given Poems for Encouragement

Copyright © 2021 by Miss Jerry Lee Schock.

Paperback ISBN: 978-1-63812-152-7
Ebook ISBN: 978-1-63812-153-4

All rights reserved. No part in this book may be produced and transmitted in any form or by any means, electronic, or mechanical, including photocopying, recording, or by any information storage and retrieval system, without permission in writing from the copyright owner.

The views expressed in this work are solely those of the author and do not necessarily reflect the views of the publisher hereby disclaims any responsibility for them.

Published by Pen Culture Solutions   01/01/2022

Pen Culture Solutions
1-888-727-7204 (USA)
1-800-950-458 (Australia)
support@penculturesolutions.com

The book *"88 God Given Poems for Encouragement."* truly inspires me a lot. You uplift me with your poems in many ways. You motivate me to keep going in life. Especially with what the world is facing right now this book gives me a lot of encouragement. I highly recommend this book to everyone.

—Alex Sanders

Contents

1. A Place of Rest 1
2. A Precious Gift 2
3. Abiding In Him 3
4. Again Lord?? 4
5. Alone but Never Lonely 5
6. Always Near 6
7. Always There 7
8. Another Storm 8
9. Another Trial 9
10. As I Pray 10
11. Barriers to Blessings 11
12. Before 12
13. Blessings 13
14. Covered Over 14
15. Father Here I Am Again 15
16. For All the Times 16
17. For Our Special Mother 17
18. From the Lord for the Hurting 19
19. God's Retirement Plan? 20
20. God's Servants 21
21. God's "Soldiers" 23
22. Gods True Servant 25
23. He Cares 26
24. He Draws Us Near 27
25. He Holds It All 28
26. Her Pain 29
27. His Healing Hands 30
28. His Promise 31
29. His Protection 32

30. His Way 33
31. His Wings 34
32. How Deep the Valley?.. 35
33. I Do Not Know 36
34. I Have Somewhat Against Thee...................................... 37
35. In the Furnace 38
36. In the Valley... 39
37. It May Be 40
38. It Seems So Soon 42
39. Life With My Sisters 43
40. More Than A Pastor 44
41. Mother 45
42. My Heart's Desire 46
43. Only the Lord Knows 47
44. Our Missionaries 48
45. Our Shelter 49
46. Out Of...... 50
47. Peace 51
48. Picking Up Stones 52
49. Praise to the Lord 54
50. Remember Others..... 55
51. Remind Me 56
52. Safe in the Storm... 57
53. So Unreal... 58
54. Someone Cares 59
55. Sometimes... 60
56. Suffering 61
57. Thank You Lord 62
58. That Desert Place 63
59. The Battle.. 64
60. The Battle Weary... 65
61. The Course Is Set.. 66
62. The Darkness 67
63. The Dove Has Landed 68
64. The Intercessor 69
65. The Intercessory Prayer 70
66. The Lord Is Watching 71
67. The Miracle in the Mirror 72
68. The Oasis 73
69. The Pain Inside 74

70. The Road 75
71. The Seeds 76
72. The Shadow of His Hand 77
73. The Son Still Shines 78
74. The Storm 79
75. The Unknown 80
76. The Valley 81
77. The Valley of Despair 82
78. The Vineyard of Our Life 83
79. Trust Him 84
80. Victory in the Valley 85
81. We Cannot Carry the Burden 86
82. What if We Knew? 87
83. When God Made the Father 88
84. When We Can Do No More 89
85. When We Cannot Understand 90
86. When You Will Not Let Me Rest 91
87. Who Is the Gospel For 92
88. Yet Another Valley 93

A Place of Rest

There is a place of quiet rest within the Saviors arms
Safety even in the storm, I am kept from harm
No one can ever know the peace flowing from above
Until they trust the Savior –and lean only on His love
He's waiting in the sunshine and even in the rain
He dries our every tear in sickness and in pain
He promises victory through our faith and as we see it grow
The Savior is protecting and watching us I know.

By Jerry L Schock
10/20/06

A Precious Gift

We have a priceless gift and we cannot see it's face
It's a gift from the Heavenly Father – His unending grace
Time cannot destroy nor mar the beauty of this gift
And through all kinds of trails – our very soul it will lift.

Jerry L Schock
08/01/2006

Abiding In Him

Abiding in the loving care of the One who knows it all,
Even when we stumble, He'll never let us fall.
He walks through every valley well before we go;
And every time a tear falls He will surely know.
The trial you are facing now has been charted from above,
The Savior went ahead for you and now carries you in love.
The road may be rough and rocky and to you it is unknown;
But rest assured my sister, you'll never walk it alone;
For Jesus stands with you to carry you through this trail-
Peace and rest will be yours in just a little while.

                from the Lord
                Jerry L Schock
                04/24/2006

Again Lord??

The valley sure is deep, the road sometimes seems long,
As I watch those around me suffer -it all seems so wrong.
And yet I know dear Lord, although it seems unfair,
You grow us up through trials and You are always there.
We walk through every valley - and try to wear a smile,
Because we know there's always glory in the trial.
But Lord my heart is aching -as once again I see,
My very precious sister, in yet another valley.
I'm praying for a miracle within Your precious will;
As she is waiting patiently, You whisper, "peace be still".
I've watched her so often, with a smile upon her face,
Father, when you made her, You sure poured on the grace.
I pray Your healing power will touch her body today;
Just one touch from Your hand.-can make pain go away.
And if there is nothing in this illness, to bring glory to You,
Then Father, please remove it -as only You can do.
You truly are the healer, when You deem that it should be;
Father-hear the prayers of your saints, let it begin with me.

II Cor. 12:9
Jerry L. Schock
2/6/00

Alone but Never Lonely

Alone but never lonely-for You the hours fill-
Hurting but not despairing-for You give a love so real.
In the valley but not alone-for You walk the road ahead,
In the middle of the storm-You remove all dread.
Father as we face life and much is unknown we fear-
Our hearts yearn for rest and we may even shed a tear.
But You will never fail us-nor leave us all alone-
Your promises are true and to us Your grace is shown.

02/25/07
Given to me by the Lord
Jerry L Schock

Sometimes when it gets too rough, I just picture the child in me crawling up into my Heavenly Father's lap. There I can find comfort and always find open arms to hold me close and love me; and He even lets me cry when I need to…but He always wipes away the tears and makes me smile before I leave there. I never want to wander too far from that place of safety where I find protection in the shelter of His wings. He gave me this poem very early one morning as I prayed for a sister in need.

Always Near

He is not waiting beyond the next hill, that we think we cannot climb,
He stands very near the child in pain, just waiting for the time,
we put our hand out to reach for His, to lead us through the storm,
And carry us through our trials, from which much faith is born.
He is not in the distant somewhere, farther than we can see,
But standing near and waiting, to wrap arms of love 'round you and me.
He feels the pain within your heart – He knows your deepest sorrow-
He's right beside you –there to help- until you can face tomorrow..
Don't try to bear the load alone, as it presses in from every side,
Go into the arms of the Father –where you can safely abide.
Lay your head upon His breast – let the Father draw you near-
Oh child the very hand of God is there , to wipe away your tears

For those who are trying to "bear up" under their burdens,

Jerry L. Schock 5/26/01

Always There

You always meet us where we are,
You come to comfort no matter how far-
You walk before us on the road of life,
And before we face the trial-already feel our strife.
You go down into the valley- deep in our despair
And You pick up the burden before we ever get there.
You always know what's lying just around the bend,
And Your vision takes You all the way to the end.
You guide us through the trials we face every day;
And continue to protect – even when we forget to pray.
Thank You Precious Father for everything You do-
Though we'll never understand the grace
that flows from You..

From the Lord for the hurting
Jerry L Schock
08/01/2006

Another Storm

I've felt the waves come crashing in and seen You calm the storm.
I've felt like I am lost and will never find my way back home.
I have felt as if the sun would surely never shine again
And then I've seen the rays of love –upon the new horizon-
I've been so low in the valley and high upon the hill-
I've led another to the Lord and felt an awesome thrill-
But as I watch storm clouds gather around loved ones so dear-
My heart cries out for them, and I ask You draw them near.
Another sister is facing a trial so unthinkable to me-
And all that I can do is pray – help her Lord I plea.
She loves You and is faithful to do Your precious will-
It's hard to know that she is in another valley still.
Oh Father will You heal her with just the touch of Your hand?
As You have so many times –Oh Lord –I know You can.

For Miss Bertha
From my heart to yours
Love & prayers
Miss Jerry
08/15/06

Miss Jerry Lee Schock

Another Trial

I cannot understand as they face another trial
Why they cannot find rest Lord for just a little while.
It seems one battle is over and another valley past-
When they are in the midst of another storm, how long will it last?
Oh Father will You heal those I've come to love so much?
As we seek Your will we still must ask for that healing touch.
We never want to stand in the way as You plan and walk ahead-
But sometimes precious Father our hearts are filled with dread.
We cannot see tomorrow and the unknown is a fearful place-
We beg for your sweet rest and pray for peace and grace.

For my sisters who face the unknown
Jerry L Schock
07/27/2006

As I Pray

I do not know the road you walk, but beside you I will be.
Nor the trials you may face but prayers are a promise from me.
I'll hold you up before the Lord as I claim His promises true,
And ask the Father in Heaven to send His angels to you.
He has walked the road before you and He finds no surprise,
The course was charted long ago, though hidden from your eyes.
And He may let you dwell in the valley to draw you closer to Him;
But you can rest assured the mountaintop is ahead for you to win.
He keeps your hand close in His own as on the road you go;
Leading you ever onward to great triumph I know.

By Jerry L. Schock
9/5/96

Barriers to Blessings

Preached at Galilean Baptist Church 12/12/10, by a premier preacher--with a premier sermon, Dr. Rex McPherson

Don't let us be the barrier to a blessing, for someone in need,
Help us to always be listening for the Holy Spirit to lead.
It may be they need a hand to help them through their day,
Or a shoulder to lean on, as they travel down life's way.
Their need may be financial or just a whispered prayer-
Something which will let them know, that we truly care.
The need may be as simple as a hug or an extended hand,
To help someone who is weary, as we follow His plan.
It may take some extra time, or money we need to spend,
But it all belongs to the Lord, it's not ours in the end.
So listen for the Spirit and ask Him to be your guide,
As you search for those in need, He's ever at your side.

Given to me by the Lord
12/13/2010
Jerry L Schock

My constant prayer-Lord help me to be what I **should** be for You,
so that I can be what I **need** to be for others.

Before

Before the trial begins or the pain is in our heart,
Before the first step into the valley draws us far apart-
Before the enemy starts the battle to bring us any pain-
The Lord has sent His angels to protect us once again.
Before we even whisper the prayer and call upon the Lord-
He has the answer on the way from His Holy Word..
His provision is always waiting for each and every need-
Before us he has walked –if only we believe.

                From the Lord for the hurting
                Jerry L Schock
                07/31/2006

Blessings

Today Lord as I ponder, the blessings I have known,
My heart is well reminded that I am never alone.
You wrap me up in arms of love, draw me close to You.
Words of praise fill my soul for everything You do.
Thanks for the love of friends and family oh so dear,
For those who dwell close to me and those far from here.
Thank You for Your precious words that cause my soul to leap,
And for every verse You've planted in my heart so deep.
Thank You for the prayer You send to intercessors minds,
That makes the path we walk here, seem a lot more kind.

By Jerry L. Schock
3/9/02

Covered Over

Covered over with prayer,
Surrounded by so much love,
From the God of all comfort-
Up in Heaven above.

No matter what I face,
No matter where I go,
I'm surrounded by His grace,
This one thing I know.

The words came from her heart
As I heard my sister say-
How very much she loved,
Knowing, that others pray.

For Martha Sweat with much love and prayer
-as you continue to draw on His strength and
the love and prayers of others.

Given to me by the Lord
6/26/11
Jerry L Schock
Is. 43:2

Father Here I Am Again

Father here I am again,
bringing other's needs to You,
How I pray You'll relieve their pain,
let them be renewed.
It seems they just move out of a valley
filled with pain,
And then we turn around-and
find them there again.
Father we can't question
the wisdom of Your way,
But we can ask You bring relief,
quickly Lord we pray.

Jerry L Schock 06/02

For All the Times

For all the times I was low in spirit and You've lifted me up,
For all the times I'm empty and You've overfilled my cup-
For all the times I felt alone and forgot how much You care-
For special loved ones You give me-who help my load to bear.
For a cross that held our Savior-between earth and sky-
For every tear I've ever shed-You've reached down to dry.
For peace flowing like a river –in the middle of the storm-
I lift my voice in praise to You-who ruleth from the throne.

From the Lord
02/25/07
Jerry L Schock

For Our Special Mother

Mommy you've gone to Heaven to meet your Savior there,
Far removed from pain, and all this earthly care.
God gave you many years –to help us learn and grow,
Filling us with love, teaching the way to go.
You taught us with a faith that time can never take away -
And said the Lord would provide each and every day.
Things were not always easy for you on the path of life-
But the faith you had in God carried you through the strife.
You always found time to play and the memories are sweet-
Remembering all the fun -like skating down the street.
We bowled and played baseball and enjoyed all we did-
As you made time for each of us- loving every kid.
We knew the time would come when we'd have to part-
What an empty place it leaves deep within our heart.

Your love surrounds us now each and every day-
And will carry us through life-helping us not to stray-
You saw us through all the heartaches life would bring-
And the I love you's that we heard- in our ears still ring.
Life's lessons have been learned in the time we had with you,

And only Heaven will reveal the rewards God has it's true-
For such a loving Mother —who sacrificed so much-
Ensuring each and every one of us felt your loving touch.

In loving memory of our Mom-
Ada L Schock
5/10/1921 to 7/19/2011
By Jerry Lee Schock
7/24/11

From the Lord for the Hurting

Oh Lord we grow so weary from the struggle of it all-
As the fiery darts of Satan 'round us we see fall.
He plans to undo our peace and plays games with our minds-
We seem to struggle daily not to get behind.
We're standing in the gap as you walk a rocky road-
The Lord sent us especially to help you bear the load.
He's walking right beside us as the journey we begin-
And rest assured He'll be there well beyond its end.
He lets us know when you're hurting or need an extra prayer-
And from the throne of Heaven sends angels waiting there.
So if you feel a touch upon your cheek today –
It's the finger of the angels, God is sending your way.

Miss Jerry L Schock

God's Retirement Plan?

What am I to do my precious Lord, Is it time to move aside?
Oh NO! Stand firm where you are my child, The Holy Spirit cried.
For there is a very special place in which you have been set,
There is no retirement plan from My work, I know you won't forget.
I remember all the promises you made when you were oh so young,
That faithfully you would serve Me, 'til it was time to come Home.
Though trials may come your way, and your body weary grows,
Stay in that place my child, for you're the only one who knows,
The valley's and the mountaintops that finally brought you here,
The way that My own hand, has dried your every tear.
Lay aside the work that I planned for only you to do?
I think not my child, it's a charge given 'specially to you.
You see, I needed someone, who would have a special faith,
And truly understand the meaning, of My unending grace.
There really is no other, and I promise to let you rest,
Once you get to Heaven, you'll enjoy with Me, the very best.

By Jerry L Schock
Given to me by the Lord
For anyone who ever thought it ws time to quit.
Copyright 01/31/1999

God's Servants

I ask You Lord what I can do to let these precious one know,
How much they are appreciated-as around the world they go!
Finding myself without words to say is so unusual for me-
Because You always let them flow like water into a sea.
Now my precious Father I search my heart, soul and mind-
Going into the deepest parts-those special words to find.
I am so very grateful they've chosen to follow Your way,
Even though many times-there is such a price to pay
Some have seen the enemy steal a loved ones peace of mind,
Others have illness and suffer loss of many different kinds.
And yet-serve on they do-without many comforts of home,
Often times they find themselves on the mission field alone.
Yet they continue to serve you with such unselfish love-
Father give them all they need here-and special rewards above.
Grant they see many saved as they labor to do Your will-
Let them feel Your Presence-as You whisper "peace be still".
In the very deepest recesses of their heart and mind-
Comfort, joy and peace for the journey, is what I pray they find-
Remind them that deep in the valley-they are never alone,

**For somewhere precious Father-prayer
brings them to the Throne.**

As you serve Him where you are called,
Remember, somewhere an intercessor listens for
His voice to touch their hearts for you needs.
Until we meet again,
Jerry L Schock
Gal. 6:2

God's "Soldiers"

Father there are those who fight a very different war,
They battle for the souls of men-some on a distant shore.
You fit them for the battle with a shield and sword,
Cover them with the armor-of Your own precious Word.
As the battle hot is raging-I stop and look around-
I see a brother falter-is he falling to the ground?
Oh Father, let me lift them up-in intercessory prayer,
Rushing to the battlefield-pull them up from there.
Keep them safe from hurt or harm-and danger here below
Wrap them in Your arms of love-and Father, let them know-
Many will be praying-when it seems the cause is lost-
Give them extra special care-as they carry Your cross.
Lord help me never to forget-not one day that I live,
How much prayer can mean to those who freely give.
The missionary, pastor, and men who are called to preach,
Nurses, helpers, singers, builders and those who teach.
Lord keep them ever before me-as prayers to Heaven rise-
Let each one find very special love and favor in Your eyes.

Given to me by the Lord
Inspired by Tolbert Moore-as he asked the

Mullins family to sing "Another Soldier Down"
and our men went to the soldiers who were
in the valley on their battlefield.
May 11, 1999-GPA Campmeeting
Jerry L Schock
Gal. 6:2

25 Years of Service

Gods True Servant

*We are at a loss for words- as we honor our Pastor today.
You've spread so much love and happiness all along the way.
Unselfishly your servant heart has taken you over this earth,
There are no words we can say to tell you what you're worth.*

*Twenty-five years you've given of self, from a heart of purest gold;
As you've preached, and spread a message that never will grow old.
You've stayed true to the Word of God as you sought to do His will-
Unchanging now, for all these years, remaining steady still.*

*You've walked through many valleys and even shed some tears
Standing only on the Word of God -man you will not fear.
We ask the Lord to bless- as you continue on the way,
With health and multiplied blessings for each and every day.*

*Galilean Baptist Church
On your 25th anniversary
Tolbert Moore
Jerry L Schock
6/1/08*

He Cares

Sometimes we look to Heaven, and cannot understand,
Within our finite minds The Master's special plan.
His sight is longer than our own, At times we cannot see;
It is then we cry to the Father, Help me Lord, we plea.
He knows our every pain and feels our deepest woe,
He cares when we are hurting and is sure to let us know.
Sometimes through a word and others through a prayer;
He sends a special one to us, just to say "I care".
Many thoughts are with you and prayers are many too.
Being sent to the Father from all of us to you;
That angels will surround you and keep you close today
Wrapped in the love of Jesus to help you on the way.

Jerry L. Schock

He Draws Us Near

If you're feeling lonely-
you are never alone;
God will draw you near to Him
from His Heavenly throne.
In the middle of the valley-
and in the hardest time-
You are His precious child,
and forever on His mind.

From the Lord
02/25/07
Jerry L Schock

He Holds It All

Thank You precious Father –when we cannot understand
That life and all it's questions, are held there in Your hand.
Thank You when it looks as if the unthinkable has come;
You take control and send Your angels to us one by one.
You give us prayer warriors, to come before the throne,
Letting those we love know, they'll never walk alone.
A brother walks an unknown path –where we're often ask to go,
Remind him Lord to praise You –for the road You surely know.
You've walked that path before Him – the way to You is clear
He's leaning close upon Your breast –please God, hold him near.
Let Him feel Your arms of love as they draw him close to You;
Grant him extra peace and comfort now –as only You can do;
And when this trial is behind him, and the answers he may know;
Oh Father, his praises will be for You –to Heaven they will go!!

Given to me by the Lord
Jerry L. Schock
8-17-99

Her Pain

Dear Lord, if I could have only one thing today,
It would be from my sister, the pain-You'd take away.
She seems to have more valleys, than anyone I've known-
Yet my precious Father- through each one she has grown.
You see- she is so very special - to those of us who look,
Upon the very heart of her - that reads like a precious book.
Her love for You is so like a perfume that is fine and rare,
And I ask today dear Father, You would grant this prayer.
As she lives her life for You - upon this earth below,
Please send her heavenly angels -to set her face aglow
And let her feel a hug - that only You can give
From the One who'll walk beside her -
every day she'll live.

With love, from the Lord to Jerry to Bertha
10/98

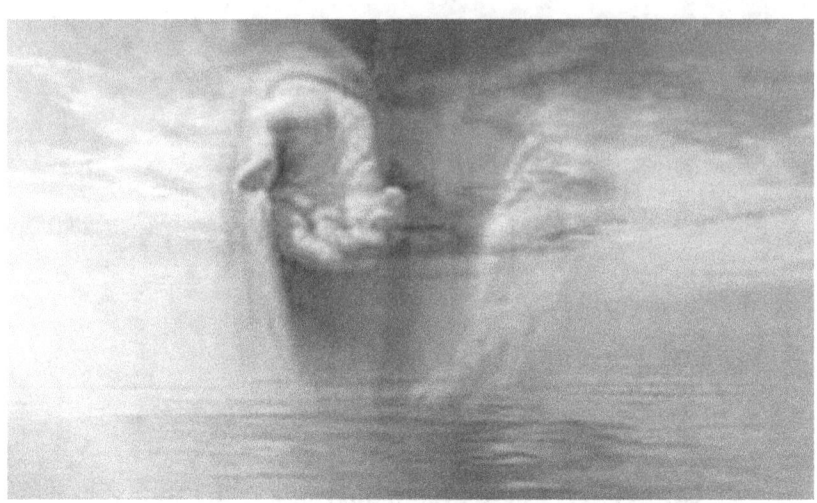

His Healing Hands

The rest, will it ever come? To those saddened hearts I see?
Yes my Father in Heaven, bring that peace I plea.
Give them peace and comfort, as they walk closely to shore,
You'd never leave them all alone – of this one thing I'm sure.
They trust each time the devil fights with some new attack
Drawing closer to Your loving heart – Father, they do not slack.
Please send those angels from Heaven to guide and to protect,
Each step they take along life's path –I know You won't forget
Father, will You ease their pain and use Your healing Hands
To soothe the brow of one who hurts-more than they can stand?
Healing the body and the hurt can only come from You
Father my prayer is You will now let the promise ring true.
As we make intercession – trusting only in Your Word;
Let the healing now begin –please grant it precious Lord

Given to me by the Lord
Jerry l Schock
12/20/98

His Promise

God made the rainbow as a promise of better things to come.
If you look very closely you'll find it when the rain is gone.
There's no way I can promise the sky will always be blue;
But rest assured His promise-will never fail to ring true.
The storm clouds ? they may gather – and they will hide the sun,
But once they've passed away, you'll find the battles won !
So many times we suffer pain, and we can't know just why,
Surely as the sun will rise tomorrow –the rainbow will be in the sky.
So look up my precious sister, good things are waiting for you,
The Father up in Heaven? His promise will always be true.

Written with love & a prayer for His healing hand to
touch you as never before.

Jerry L. Schock
12-7-98
Gal. 6:2

His Protection

The valley may seem so deep, sometimes you may feel alone;
But the Father up in Heaven, knows the path you're on.
He sees each rock and stony place, upon the road ahead;
He's gone ahead before you, so you will not have to dread.
He's surrounding you with angels, to protect you on the way;
And send His peace and comfort – for facing each new day.
The prayers of many follow you, no matter where you go;
And the Father loves you dearly, in the Bible, it tells you so.
So my prayer, my precious sister, is for peace as you go on,
And somehow He will let you know, you'll never be alone.
He's wrapped His arms around you, to keep you in His care;
And no matter where you are, may you feel His presence there.

Given to me by the Lord,

12-98
Jerry Schock

Gal. 6:2 "Bear ye one another's burdens and so fulfill the Law of Christ."

His Way

Lord, what am I supposed to do -when others suffer so?
You've given me a heart for those who are feeling low.
How much deeper in the valley? How much lower can they go?
Father the night closes in - they may not be sure You know!
Faith waivers when we see loved ones face yet another trial.
Will You give sweet rest to them, for just a little while?
Help them as they travel yet another road unknown,
To understand You've been there -and they are not alone
Let them the feel the prayers of the intercessors You've given;
As daily we come before Your throne -reaching up to Heaven.
Help them realize although the way seems dark and drear,
That You control all things -and will dry their every tear..
Someday You may choose to let us understand –
But until then my precious Lord-
protect them with Your own hand.

Gal. 6:2 "Bear ye one another's burdens and so fulfill the Law of Christ."
Jerry L. Schock

His Wings

Under the shadow
of His wings –
Is where I want to be,
Resting in the loving care
- of the One I long to see.
No fear can rise
nor foe abide
As safely beneath
His wings I hide.

Given to me by the Lord
Jerry L Schock
8-16-02

How Deep the Valley?

The valley seems so deep Lord, will it ever end
Yes my precious child, you will feel whole again.
I know the pain you feel and see the tears you cry,
But my promises are true, each teardrop I will dry.
I'm with you in the valley –you are not on your own-
For in My Word I've promised, you'll never be alone.
I'll carry you through this valley as I have in the past,
When we're through the valley, peace will come at last.
I never promised roses or a life without any pain,
But in the end, My child, you'll be the one to gain.
Your Mama's safe in Heaven and waiting here for you,
Along with many loved ones, who are waiting too.

Given to me by the Lord for the Moore Family Jerry L Schock
12/27/10

I Do Not Know

I do not know what you face or the road that you must take
But I know the Father in Heaven —cannot make a mistake.
No trials can come our way —or touch us in this place
Except it first is approved -above-at the Throne of Grace.
So when the road is hard to walk and the pain you cannot bear-
Know the Father in Heaven, cares and is always there.
He walked the road before you and knows each step ahead-
Hold on my precious loved one-there is nothing you should dread.
Hold that precious promise in your heart that you'll never be alone-
And take the burdens to the Lord-lay them at the throne.

By Jerry L. Schock

"...I Have Somewhat Against Thee"

From God's Word-"...I have somewhat against thee" –
I heard the Preacher say.
Within my heart I asked the Lord –what should I see today?
The Bible tells us to judge ourselves as we journey through this life-
By obeying His Word and inspecting self-we can avoid much strife.

The Spirit quickly reveals to us, things not pleasing to the Lord-
If we'll listen very prayerfully, to the preaching of the Word.
He prepares the heart of the Preacher –through many hours of prayer-
And as the Word is delivered to us,-we can see the depth of His care.

"..I have somewhat against thee"-Lord what do I need to do,
To make my life and testimony –a blessing to others for You?
I asked You Lord to open my eyes so inside myself I can see-
Things that need confession Lord-to be what I should be.

Help me to be what I should be for You Lord as I walk the road ahead-
So that I can be what I need to be for others –with no fear or dread.
Make me a vessel of honor so when before You I stand-
The words "...I have somewhat against thee"
will never be heard again.

Inspired by a sermon preached at Galilean Baptist Church
by Dr. Rex McPherson on June 5, 2011
Given to me by the Lord
Jerry L Schock

Rev. 2:4 "Nevertheless I have somewhat against thee,
because thou hast left thy first love."

In the Furnace

In the furnace of affliction-many times I see
The mighty hand of God refining you and me
He lets us feel the pressure and often times the flame
But never will they harm us – we will always gain
He works us like fine silver heated to refine
The test sometimes seem endless-but the victory is mine
I see a glow in the trial as the heat begins to rise
There is a rainbow in the clouds and sunlight in the skies
And though I'm in the furnace, His love begins to show
As through the heat I will emerge with my face aglow

By Jerry L Schock
10/20/06

In the Valley

In the valley you are walking, though it may seem dark and dim;
You know the Lord is near you, as you're reaching out for Him.
He knows each doubt and fear, and sees each tear you cry,
He's placed angels all around you, to protect as days go by;
He's walked the road before you and already bore the pain,
You'll grow through trials you're facing; you'll be the one to gain.
All within the Lords good time, the valley dim will be,
As you're looking down from the mountain and know,
His grace is sufficient for thee.

5/30/97
given to me by the Lord
Jerry L. Schock
II Cor. 12:9

It May Be

*Inspired by a sermon preached at Galilean Baptist Church
National GPA Campmeeting, June 4,2012
by Delmar Duvall from Jeremiah 36*

God said,
It may be, they will hear and return from their evil way,
And He is so willing to forgive, if only we will pray.
When we fail to heed the words given to the man of God-
And choose the wrong path to take, we feel the chastening rod.
And if we cut out Godly things from the life we've been given,
We will surely break the heart, of our Father, up in Heaven.
If we have no fear of the Lord, and choose the world instead,
We are sure to find discontent, on the road ahead.
It may be –God is seeking-and His Word will forever ring true,
Surely if we will listen, blessings wait for me and you.
But if, as it were in days of old, we fail to heed God's Word,
We risk the wrath and anger of our precious Lord.
It may be -the road will not be so long, if God's way we choose-
It may be –the trial will pass us-there is so much to lose-

The God of second chances, He sends the messenger near,
Asking only that we listen, and heed the words we hear.
It may be- today -if you choose God's way instead,
Peace and comfort will be yours on the journey ahead.

>Given to me by the Lord
>Jerry L Schock
>6/4/12

It Seems So Soon

It seems too soon my brother, for you to be going Home,
But we pray your crossing is easy –and know you'll not be alone.
For Jesus is waiting on the other side –to take you safely there,
To a place with no more pain or sorrows and never any care.
We hate to let you go now but we know it is in God's time-
And we would not have you suffer –even though we're left behind.
You're leaving us such sweet memories of good times we have shared,
And the thing we'll remember most, is just how much you've cared.
We will miss your great hugs each time we would meet-
All the conversations we shared and then that smile so sweet.
Our one true consolation is that we had love to share-
And know that someday in Heaven we'll all be meeting there.

For our sweet brother Roy,
as we wait on the Lord.
Jerry L Schock
10/12/14

Thank you Lord for letting me hear his voice today and tell him how much I love him - and hear him say I love you too sis-like he always did. You let me read this poem to him. Even though he is weak Lord-You sustain life until You are ready to come for him.

Life With My Sisters

Life brings unexpected blessings, as we travel on our way.
Mine has been my Sisters, each and Every day.
We've shared both pain and sorrow,
And laughs along the way.
Ollie and Linda, Lessie and Jane.
We shared the happy times and even bore the pain.
We have depended fully on the Lord.
And trusted in His Word.
Through good times and through bad,
Always we did gain.
There is No way to say-How Special you are to me.
And Daily as I pray-for Him to meet the needs.
I ask Him to protect you all
As on His name you call.

I love you ALL,
More than you can EVER know.

Your Sister,
Jerry Lee
Ecc 3:1

More Than A Pastor

You are more than a Pastor and much more than a friend
You pray for and look after the flock and love us without end.
You seek the will of God for all you have to do
And trust so much in the plans and things He has for you.
You've never failed to preach the Word –
and stay close to His own heart.
Vowing not to stray or from His will depart.
Only up in Heaven will the results of your service be known
So until we get to Heaven-I'll thank you on my own.
Thanks for all the prayers and all the sermons true-
For sharing many of the visions God has given you.
For giving of yourself and not asking for any return-
For showing God's love so freely as for lost souls you yearn.
Thank you my dear Pastor for everything you do
And let me say with love- Happy Father's Day to you.

> Love and prayers
> Miss Jerry
> 2006

Mother

We needed someone to lead us and guide us on the way,
One who could take us –through even the hardest day.
So God made that special someone who is like no other;
This blessing we've been given –He chose to call our Mother.
She seems to have an answer to every question we ask,
And never seems to tire-no matter how hard the task.
Sometimes she's a nurse-who treats our hurts and pain-
At other times she's a manager without a thing to gain.
Sometimes she's a maid or cook –it seems there is no end-
But always she is the one on whom we can depend.
She does not demand any wages and her schedule is not set-
She serves at the oddest hours and never seems to forget.
She lives to serve her family and has a very full life-
Being a Mother and a friend and also being a wife.
She loves the Lord and church –knows many hymns by heart.
She's always ready to serve no matter how small the part.
Today is the time to honor, God's special gift from above-
By giving back to our Mother's, an extra measure of love.

Mothers Day -2007
Jerry L Schock

My Heart's Desire

No matter where I walk in this world Lord, I know You walk with me,
Down the roughest road, up the steepest hill, into the darkest valley.
In Your Word You give the promise, I will never be alone;
Dear Lord I trust and have the faith, not to be left on my own.
Comfort now my heart does yearn to bring to those who hurt;
And Lord the only hope I have is giving them Your Word.
My heart aches as I see a sister in Christ who bears a heavy load,
Or a brother who has fallen as he walks along life's road.
Dear Lord I pray for wisdom I walk this narrow way,
To give the help to those who need a helping hand today.
Give me the words you'd have me say, to give to them dear Lord,
Give comfort You would have me give for Your precious Holy Word.
Give me the wisdom Lord I need to lend a helping hand today;
To those who hurt and feel the pain, walking down life's way.
Lord I want to be a comfort and a help in time of need,
I want always to give to others in thought and word and deed.

10/5/95
Gal. 6:2
Jerry L. Schock

Only the Lord Knows

Who knows the pain that a parent feels when a child has gone astray,
Or the emptiness within our arms, when someone goes away?
Who knows the lonely nights we have when we bury a loved one dear,
Or the ache we feel so deep inside wanting to hold them near.
Who knows the anguish that we feel when others suffer pain,
And try as we may we cannot see a way for them to gain?
Who knows the nights we spend in prayer at the throne of grace,
Or the many times we're led, intercession to make?
Only God has the answers to all the questions at hand
He did not leave the answers to us, as fallen man.
But He's given us wisdom to know, we are always in His care,
No matter what the problem or trial, our Lord is always there.
Even when our faith will falter, and our spirit is so low,
We know He has the answers, it is to Him we should go.
He's waiting there, with open arms, no matter what the care–
Saying welcome home My child – I've been waiting here.
Though I may not reveal to You all the answers today,
Snuggle up real close to me–I'll love your cares away.

For those who just do not know...
He has the answers...
By JERRY L SCHOCK 6/29/00

Our Missionaries

Here I am again Lord bringing them to You in prayer,
Asking only that You would remove their care.
Many changes await them on the journey they make;
Father give them wisdom as this road they take.
I know that many hours and maybe even tears-
Have been spent with You pouring out their fears.
Change is never easy and yet You promise to go ahead,
And make the journey before us-removing so much dread.
Father their hearts desire has always been to serve,
Deep within their souls -they know-it's what You deserve.
Build up high that hedge of thorns,
From the enemy – please protect.
When the night is dark or the road is rough-
Remind them –to pray, we won't forget.

For Brother Dennis and Miss Amelia,
As you begin a new journey in your service for Him,
Under the shadow of His protection.
With love & prayers,
Miss Jerry
Psalm 91

Our Shelter

You truly are the lighthouse, that we seek in every storm,
The only safety we can find –and protection from all harm.
That beacon shines so brightly in the middle of the night
When we are trembling with fear, You send to us the Light.
We know the ship is battered and at times the sails are torn,
And yet my Lord you've promised shelter from the storm.
Our faith will often falter in the storm, forgive us Lord we pray,
As you bring us though the waves so high, into the light of day.
Thank You for being the lighthouse shining from the shore,
Thank for the promise of peace and love with You forevermore.

Given to me by the Lord
3-01
Jerry L. Schock

Out Of......

Out of trials come triumph,
Peace from sorrow and woe.
Out of tears the sunshine
As through this life we go.
Out of pain comes patience
And a faith that will ascend,
To the Father up in Heaven
On the wings of prayer without end.
We want to send our wishes
And prayers across the miles,
And hope the smallest thought
Will bring you hours of smiles.
Rest assured our Father in Heaven
Has angels around you today.
And He is guiding you through
Every step of the way.

By Jerry L. Schock

Peace

Promises from Heaven that time cannot destroy-

   Even in the valley He comes to bring us joy-

     All the while we're facing each and every trial

Calm He gives in the midst of the storm to restore our smile

   Every promise from Heaven forever to be claimed

-from the Father above until peace and joy shall reign.

given to me by the Lord for the hurting
Jerry L Schock
08/05/2006

Inspired by a sermon preached at the National GPA Camp meeting 06/08/10 by Don Jackson

He said we have a field called our past, filled with the stones of life's experiences, and not to complain if we choose to pick up stones made from bad experiences.

Picking Up Stones

For everything we experience in life another stone is laid, Each time we fail or triumph for every decision we've made. For every hurt or victory, each heartache, and each smile; And there will be a multitude of stones in just a little while.

We lay good stones for our salvation, or studying God's Word. For each soul we lead to Him and blessings from the Lord. Bad ones for disappointments and friends who break our heart For wrong choices we have made or from God's way we part.

It is our choice to pick them up, both the good and bad; Picking up stones of regret will surely make us sad. If we carry them for too long the load is hard to bear- It will surely leave us weak, filled with sorrow and care

*By picking up stones of joy and happy memories made- Peace
begins to flow within –a different foundation is laid.
We then begin to praise God, showing forth His love.
Lay good stones in the field of life, thank the Lord above*

*Stones have no power of their own-take care which you choose-
If you hold onto a bad one too long, surely your joy you'll lose.
Our choices will give them power and trouble we quickly find'- If
the good ones we have chosen as the ones to leave behind.*

*Given to me by the Lord,
Jerry L Schock
06/11/10*

Praise to the Lord

As we look at Your creation and You draw us ever near,
Even in the face of death, there is still no need to fear.
Your promise is to keep us, no matter how dark the night,
And down in the lowest valley, we know You are the light.
Lord you know our hearts are breaking for a loved one in pain,
You may even hear us question You, what is there to gain?
But You can see much farther than we will ever see,
You plan each step along the way –help us Lord we plea.
If we can praise You today-even in the midst of the storm,
Soon we'll find that comfort and safety from all harm.

For Wayne and the family
as we wait on the Lord,
From the Lord with love
Jerry L Schock
8/2/08

Remember Others....

Oh Father up in Heaven, sometimes the path is rough,
And often times I stumble when things become too tough.
Sometimes my faith will falter and I forget for just a while,
The promises You've made, but then I remember, and smile.
You promised never to leave your children on their own,
And when we are the weakest, that's when You are so strong.
Father help me on the path of life where You've set my feet,
That I will become a blessing to everyone I meet.
Help me focus on the needs of others, so I forget my own,
Help me to pray so faithfully, they'll know they're not alone.
Let me be a prayer warrior, who never will lose sight,
Of who You are and what I'm to do as I pray with all my might.

8/5/00
Jerry L Schock

Remind Me

When I'm not sure of the outcome and my heart begins to fear,
Remind me Lord-it's in Your control-that I just need draw near.
When I've gotten out of focus-and seem to lose my way-
Remind me about praising You-and Lord help me to pray.
When I feel defeated and unsure of what to do-
Remind me to draw nearer and put my trust in You-
Help me to remember You always know what's best-
Remind me precious Father- in You I will find rest.

And I if I be lifted up He said, will draw all men to me....
Jerry Schock
02/25/07

Inspired by Wayne Sweat's Sunday School lesson on being saved
for the Lord to draw us nearer to Himself.

Safe in the Storm

The waters may be raging and the storm clouds bring alarm-
But you are safe in Jesus' care –from any and all harm
The raging storm around you –will come to an end-
The Father will carry you through –on Him you can depend.
His peace will soon be 'round you-though it escapes you now-
And His care will bring you out of the raging storm somehow.
He knows the path you are traveling – for He prepared the way.
He promises He'll not forsake you-you're not in the storm to stay.
Hold on my precious friend – trusting only in the Lord-
And you'll find yourself in the sunlight again-
According to His Word.

Psalms 107:29 He maketh the storm a calm,
so that the waves thereof are still
Hebrews 13:5 ... for he hath said, I will never
leave thee, nor forsake thee.

For those in the storm
Jerry L Schock
08/15/06

So Unreal

It all seems so unreal, as we are running through life's race;
The thought of a loved one in pain, with a smile upon her face.
She has a strength - Heaven sent - for each new burden she'll bear
And she is blessed with people, who really, truly care.
She is surrounded with angels, as she goes along life's way;
And finds comfort, as will you, in the prayers others pray
The sun will be shining - as rain makes things in the valley grow,
He knows your heart is yearning - for peace and comfort, I know.
He's been there through each trial, and He has never failed you yet;
You know our Heavenly Father, unlike us, never will forget.
He promises there'll be sunshine, after every storm we see;
His eye is on the sparrow, and He cares for you and me.
Peace is just around the corner, even though you now may doubt;
And in just a little while, from the valley, He'll lead you out.
But while you rest in the valley, know that He is near;
His own great Hand is drying, each and every tear.
He sees every burden, He allows to come your way;
As He is watching over you, each minute of the day.
Hold on My precious child, I can almost hear Him say;
The mountaintop is near, it isn't far away;
I'm walking right beside you, you will never walk alone,
Oh no, My precious child, I'll not leave you on your own!!

with much love and prayer
Jerry L Schock
7-25-98

Someone Cares

Sometimes I know you're weary and you tire along life's way,
Often you may be hurting and can't find the words to pray-
Life has dealt some hard blows on your journey here below-
But thank the Lord when we get home - there'll be no pain I know.
As family and loved ones stray from the Lord and His precious will-
And others are taken from you –and in death they lie so still-
As you watch those around you who just don't seem to care,
But still they "have it all" – and "success" surrounds them there-
You grow so weary of trying to do what you know is right-
To go on the living for the Lord –you're surrounded by the night-
You think you will go your own way and do what you want to do-
Not even depending upon the Lord and what He has for you.
But hold on my precious friend –intercessors are on every side-
Standing in the gap for you –praying in His love you'll abide.
Later down the road– when the pain is not so hard to bear–
You'll realize my precious friend –the Father has always been near.
He supplied the measure of peace you never thought you'd find-
As you walked through the valley – hurt, heavy on your mind-
He was there to hold and comfort you when tears flowed like rain-
And in your darkest hours – it was the Heavenly Father who came.
Even when the storm was raging He sent angels from above.
Wrapped His arms around you – and sheltered you with His love.

Given to me by the Lord
Jerry L Schock
04/13/04

Remember when it all seems unbearable and the world is closing in around you-that somewhere- God touches an intercessor to carry your needs to the throne room.

You are all loved very much and many prayers go Heavenward that you may never know about-God awakens us in the night or brings you to our thought during the day – and we stop and pray - trusting our Lord to send His angels to you at that very moment.. The next time you feel that sweet calm touch your soul in the midst of turmoil and trouble – just stop and think – "He's touched an intercessor somewhere just for me."

Sometimes

Sometimes the thoughts I think
Are not pleasing to my Lord-
When I am discouraged and
forget promises in His Word.
But then soon the Holy Spirit
convicts my aching soul-
The Lord sends the deepest joy
and once again I'm whole.
Thank You for the valleys
You allow me to walk thru-
As You remind me Lord-
even in bad times-
all praise belongs to You.

From the Lord
02/25/07
Jerry L Schock

Suffering

Father I must confess I simply do not understand-
How some of Your children suffer time and time again-
I am so amazed but still I know You have a Master Plan-
And no one can handle this-but Lord -I know You can.
The burden is weighing heavy tonight –for those I love so much
And my very soul cries out to You- for a special healing touch.
It's all within Your precious hands-as You manifest Your will-
Father our hearts are breaking – but trust in You we will.
Time and again on bended knee -we've brought them to the throne
With Your words ringing in our hearts-"I"ll not leave you alone"
Pour on an extra measure of grace –and peace that will abound
With many of Your angels – our loved ones please surround

09/08/06
for Bertha and Dianne and family

Thank You Lord

Thank You Lord for all the love, You put within my heart,
And touch me then, to give it away, to others as a part
Of the reward for things that I would do, unworthy as I am;
You bless me more than words can say, time and time again.
Oh Lord, I stand in awe as I behold the things You give,
As I give away what You've given me, and for You I try to live.
How often Lord, to You I come and forgiveness I must ask
As I fail and fall so very short as You assign each task.
Even in the midst of turmoil Lord, You let me feel at ease,
And still today, my heart is full, my spirit is at peace.

09/05/96
Jerry L. Schock

That Desert Place

A dry desert place- yet not alone.
Father, I feel so far from You
and the safety of 'home'
I wander along from day to day,
Sometimes not even stopping to pray
My heart cries out to You,
Oh help me Father I plea-
How much I am longing to be
What you want me to be.
Then a Hand reaches out to draw me close
And show me how much You care
You show me again Your will so true
—and I know I'm almost there.
No longer in a desert place,
but close to the Father I love.
And safely resting in Your arms-
-I feel that touch from above.

Given to me by the Lord
05/15/05
Jerry Lee Schock

The Battle

*Tho' the battle may be raging –
there is nothing I should dread,
As long as He is in control –
there's victory up ahead.
Though sometimes I am walking
in a valley low and dim,
My heart can still rejoice
and find sweet peace in Him.
For nothing here can harm me –
His promises are true,
My friend, don't ever lose hope,
He'll do the same for you.
Joy cometh in the morning,
I read in God's own word,
And never a sweeter message,
will ever again be heard.
Look upward to the greatest source of light
you'll ever see,
He will never leave or forsake us –
His love and grace are free.*

*Given to me by the Lord
12-30-98
Jerry L. Schock*

The Battle Weary

Many will come thirsty from the battle,
and weary from the fight;
But Lord, Your strength is sufficient
to give to each some light.
Your promise is to be nigh to those
with a broken heart
And many coming here Lord,
have been torn apart-
They have a vision for the lost
and dying soul today-

But the enemy would defeat
and just get in the way.
They may be weary now but with
all You will provide-
They can return to the battle
and in Your strength abide.
Help us to pray and place each one
in Your Precious Hand-
Give them what they need for battle
in a dry and thirsty land.
Let them feel Your touch as You
heal the wounded heart-
And raise the spirits of each one-
as from this oasis they depart.

For our missionaries and pastors –
as you fight the battle to win lost souls to Christ.

Love & prayers,
Miss Jerry L Schock
Galilean Baptist Church
2007 Campmeeting

The Course Is Set

Faith means that we must trust Him, when we can't see a way,
It means that we must walk with Him, each and every day.
At times we will not understand the turns our lives will take;
But we must keep the faith in Him who no mistake can make.
Oft' times He leads us down a road that seems so dark and drear;
Even then we must trust in Him and know He's ever near.
The path you walk is yet unknown, but He knows what lies ahead;
He has the future in His hands and we must never dread.
The road that you are walking now may seem strange to you,
But the Father up in Heaven has charted the course its true.
He knows each stone along the way and every crooked place
He'll carry you and be ever close in everything you face.
He's assigned you each an angel to keep you in their care;
And you can rest assured the Father always will be there.

Jerry L. Schock

The Darkness

Walking through the darkness,
we cannot understand,
We cry out in despair and reach
out for His hand.
God's purpose is for us to grow
and learn from the trials,
But in the midst of darkness-at times
we lose our smiles.
God prepares us in the darkness for
what He'd have us know,
And in the light of day-the blessings
begin to flow.
If we submit to His will in darkness,
we can learn and grow;
And obey Him so when the daylight comes-
His glory we can show.

Inspired by Charles Stanley's sermon
For Cindy
Jerry L Schock

The Dove Has Landed

Once the dove has landed, there's no question in the mind,
For the claim the Holy Spirit makes is truly one of a kind.
No need for one to wonder, for the Dove brings a special touch,
The testimony left behind –is desired so very much.
Just as the Heavenly Father sent the Dove to His own Son,
He claims His children through the Spirit, each and every one.
The Spirit bears the witness –to whom we do belong,
And with that comes a promise –we are never left alone.
Our Father promised long ago, through the words of His own Son,
That when He left this world, the Comforter would come.
True to every promise, our Father has ever made,
The peace of the Holy Spirit, upon each of us is laid.

Given to me by the Lord
Jerry L Schock
Inspired by a sermon preached by Dr. Tolbert Moore
At Galilean Baptist Church Oct. 28, 2012

The Intercessor

Making sweet intercession-for all needs
great and small.
Trusting in God's wisdom-as on His
Name we call.
Lean not to thine own understanding –
trust only in the Lord-
And He will prepare all hearts,
according to His Word.
Standing in the gap we ask the Father
to meet your every need
To send wisdom and protection
from above
–as we pray and plead.

Given to me by the Lord
Jerry L Schock
Proverbs 3:5 9/16/06

The Intercessory Prayer

My heart carries prayers to you - from the Father above,
Prayers for your un-ending peace, wrapped up in His love.
Hugs and smiles and love, beyond all you can believe,
Until the Father surely, will all your pain relieve?
Prayers for your healing, and a touch from God's own hand;
Prayers for your family, as they dwell in the valley land-
Intercessory prayer, that sweet relief will bring,
And deep within your heart, a special song you sing
The victory is coming, even though at times, it looks dim,
Because you've placed your faith and all your hope - in Him.
Your testimony all your life, has always been so sweet,
As you have trusted the Savior, every need to meet
Hold on my precious sister, as the prayers to Heaven go,
His strength and love will keep you - through anything, I know.

Jerry L. Schock

The Lord Is Watching

The Lord is watching over you, even though times are bad;
He feels the pain you're feeling and knows when you are sad.
He has placed angels all around you, to linger very near;
They will protect you and help whenever you feel fear.
The road you see ahead, to you is still unknown;
But all that you are facing has gone before the throne.
The Savior has approved it as He allows this test;
But please don't ever forget He has also promised rest.
The valley may seem more than you feel you can bear;
But He is saying rest My child, you know how much I care.
He surrounded you with others who love, care and pray,
The darkest hour's just before dawn, you're not in this valley to stay.

psalm 91
Jerry L Schock

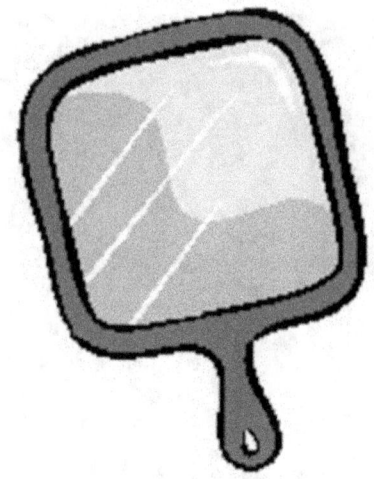

The Miracle in the Mirror

As I look into the mirror, I'm amazed at what I see-
The miracle I see today, I thank You Lord, is me.
The doctor's gave up hope, no healing they would say-
But they are not in control of life, at the end of any day.
Ye have not because ye ask not, I read in His Word-
And when He answers we give praise, only to the Lord.
Many prayers were sent to Heaven, asking Him to heal,
The Lord would answer all of them –according to His will.
If you're walking in a valley and no daylight you can see-
Leave it in the hands of God, for He loves you and me.
You may be the next miracle He chooses to perform,
As He heals a broken body and keeps you safe from harm.

Written for Crystal Swanson
From Louise Hutto
12/12/10

The Oasis

A time of sweet refreshing-as many come in from the storm,
Some are weak and weary-many are battle worn.
But in the midst of the turmoil, raging through the night,
You bring them to an oasis to refresh them in the light.
Sometimes they grow weary on the battlefield oh Lord,
Cast down by the enemy, as they spread Your precious Word.
Remind them Lord when it seems as if the enemy won the fight-
Intercessory prayer will follow them, 'til they can see the light.
Touch our hearts dear Lord, for those who are called to go-
To ever hold them up in prayer-how we love them so.

Thank You Lord for a Pastor, Tolbert Moore, who has a vision for
Campmeeting. An oasis for all those who need refreshing
to refit them for the battle.

By Jerry L Schock
08/03/2003

The Pain Inside

*Sometimes the pain goes so deep, and we hide it somewhere inside,
Refusing to let those around us see, the many tears we've cried. But somewhere in the dark of night when we cannot go on alone,
We must realize our Father in Heaven, will not leave us on our own.
He carries us through the valley, as our feet stumble on the way-
He knows what is in our hearts, when we cannot even pray.
He feels the pain and loneliness as another loved one goes home,
And promises to be very close to us, we are never alone.
When the hurt is more than I can bear, and I want to go and hide,
I must seek my Savior then —and draw closer to His side.
In His arms I can find peace, comfort and sweet rest- And know that I can lay my head, down upon His breast. I know He'll hold me in His arms and every tear He'll dry, Once I've drawn close to Him-there'll be no need to cry.*

*Given to me by the Lord 6/1/12
as I walk out of the valley of grief from the homegoing of my best friend, my Mother
Jerry L Schock*

Psalm 34:18
"The LORD is nigh unto them that are of a broken heart..."

The Road

When we walk a road that seems as if tough times will never end,
When we find ourselves hurt and alone, it seems without a friend.
When there's no where else that we can go, for comfort in our pain;
It's then that we look back, and seek our Savior once again.
Many times I asked why we wait until things have gotten so bad;
To go to the Savior and petition His help, the best friend we ever had!
When, if we had walked the path with Him, as a companion all along;
The pain would be easier to bear, in our heart's we'd have a song.
We are never ask to walk a road, or taste of a bitter cup
That He is not there, through each trial, to care and lift up

Jerry L. Schock

The Seeds

If you plant a seed in the ground and give it a little care
The Lord will water and you can see the fruit it comes to bear..
As we go through this life-we plant seeds along the way-
Some are blessings to others –but for some we'll dearly pay.
Some we plant will bring forth a beauty for all to see-
Seeds of love and kindness –that will last for eternity.
But those planted in bitterness and anger
can only bring us woe-
So be careful of the seeds you plant-
On your journey here below.

Written at the request of
Mrs. Joe Chapman
By Jerry L Schock
3/21/04

Miss Jerry Lee Schock

The Shadow of His Hand

Sometimes we walk in sunlight, others in shadows so dim;
But it's there within the shadows; we learn to listen to Him.
He covers us ever so closely, with the shadow of His hand;
As we are asked to dwell for a while, in a dry and thirsty land.
It is deep in the darkest shadows, we are able to hear His voice,
That beckons us to walk with Him, making Him our choice.
So as you dwell, my precious brother, in a valley dark and drear;
Know that His hand of protection and love is hovering very near.

Jerry L. Schock Given to me by the Lord .
3-16-97

The Son Still Shines

Just over the horizon, the sky is always blue,
The Son is always shining, no matter what we do.
His healing touch is waiting, if only we will ask;
Nothing for the Father, is too great a task.
His heart is hurting with us, as through the valley we go,
For He feels our every pain, and will comfort us we know.
Sometimes through a touch, or maybe through a prayer,
Always, He will let us know, truly He does care.
We may feel alone in the valley, but then we see the Son;
Shining through the clouds, when the day is done.
He loves you in the valley, or when you're at your best,
He longs to end the hurt, and give to you sweet rest.
Yes the Son is always shining; the sky is always blue;
Even through the clouds He's reaching out to you.
So reach up my precious sister, just give Him your hand,
Let Him wrap His arms around you-as at His side, you stand.

As the Son shines on you.
Jerry L. Schock
2/06/00

Miss Jerry Lee Schock

The Storm

The winds have raged around us and the waters overflow.
The fury of all nature –has destroyed all we know.
The outcome looks about as bleak as we have ever seen-
Oh Lord we cry out in the night –we don't know what it means.
Yet somewhere from above the storm –the Lord is watching all
Nothing has escaped His eye –of what on earth does fall.
We read all things work together for good, in His Holy Word-
But as we look around us –we could even doubt the Lord.
Hang on my precious children – For I'll make no mistake
Echo's through the destruction –as the day begins to break.
Someday you will understand – but today I ask for trust-
Wait and see what I will do – My child –it is a must.
Use the faith I gave you when you were but a child-
Don't let your mind go wandering somewhere in the wild.
Just stay close beside Me – and let Me take care of it all-
I've walked the road before you – I will bear you up-
If on My Name you'll call.

10/01/05
Jerry L Schock

The Unknown

I wonder as I watch her walk, on another path unknown,
Are there times dear Lord, my sister feels alone?
Does she know the burden is not hers, it belongs to You?
As she reaches out to Heaven-for promises so true.
I know she has strength from the many trials she's faced,
She 's rested oh so many times. On Your unchanging grace.
But Father, when the load is heavy and seems too much to bear
Many times we falter –and might forget You're there.
My prayer for her today is grace that does abound
As my precious sister –with angels You surround.
Any time she falters –and her strength becomes so weak
Touch her precious Father –as to her heart You speak.
Let her know that somewhere –in the stillness of the night;
Prayers are going upward-for You to send the light.
Let her know the burdens –are never hers alone.
Somewhere, an intercessor –claims them for their own.

Jerry L. Schock
11-1-99
Gal. 6:2

Miss Jerry Lee Schock

The Valley

Each time I'm in the valley and feeling so alone-
The Father gently whispers to me from His throne.
He whispers peace and comfort and quickly lets me know
The burden is not mine to carry – but to Him it must go.
He was in the valley before the dark clouds came my way
And He promises I am not in this valley to stay.
I look and see the mountaintop and sunshine in the sky
So quickly the storm clouds pass before I can even ask why.
Peace is in that valley and my faith He will restore-
And carry me to the sunlight where I see His grace once more.

For those
In the valley
Jerry L Schock
8/5/2006

The Valley of Despair

God picked out a valley and though it's wide and deep
I know the Heavenly Father-His promises will keep.
In the midst of the valley we cry out in despair-
But the Father has gone ahead and always will be there.
It is testing for a time and we often wonder why-
We question the Master's plan —and for peace we cry.
In the midst of the deepest valley things are lush and green-
The Father has promised while there-we can be serene.
His peace can surround us as He holds us very near-
Remember as you walk through that valley-
there is no need to fear.

For Rick Forrest- from my heart-with much prayer
As you are asked to walk through another valley-
Remember there are intercessors and God hears
Every prayer sent to throne for you-and
Most of all my precious brother-
God still answers prayer.

Love
Miss Jerry
8/15/2006

The Vineyard of Our Life

As the Lord walks by the vineyard of your life-
what is it He will see,
Overgrowth and disrepair from lack of care –oh me!
If we fail to care for our soul and feed it every day-
It begins to look to others-as if we've moved away.
For each day we must have a special time of prayer-
It is a must to let the Father know how much we care.
We must spend time in the Bible –so He our souls can feed-
And we can hear the Holy Spirit and always follow His Lead.
Witnessing to others is not optional in a Christian's life-
By sharing His love –we bring glory & honor to Jesus Christ.
If we fail to follow His daily plan -we will sink in deep despair-
And the vineyard of our life will quickly show the lack of care.

Inspired by a sermon preached at
Galilean Baptist Church
6/9/11 at Campmeeting.
By Terry McMillian
Given to me by the Lord
Jerry L Schock

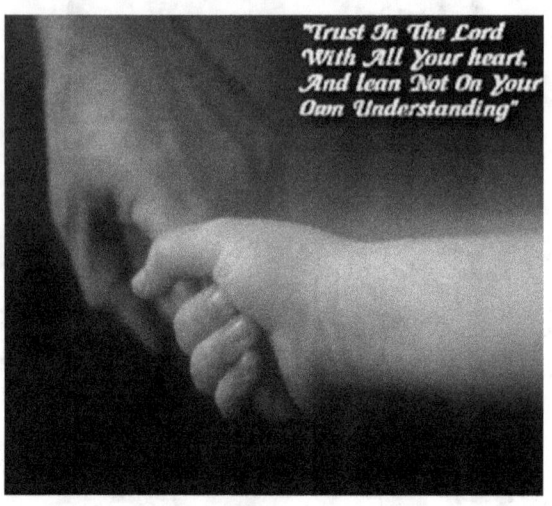

Trust Him

Often times dear Lord I wonder, is the pain too hard to bear?
But then my heart remembers just how much You really care.
You truly will be near to those with a broken heart,
Who stand by so helpless, when from loved ones they must part.
Those who suffer illness for which there is no cure-
Those who may be lonely-but of this one thing I'm sure-
No burden is too heavy, when we give the load to You,
No pain will ever to be too great -Your promises are true.
No valley is too deep - no river will be too wide ,
When we place our trust in You -and walk close to Your side.
You'll touch a prayer warrior who will begin to pray,
To carry the burdens of others through the hardest day.

For those in my church family I see suffer time and again
Jerry L. Schock

Victory in the Valley

Walking through this life, many things are there to face,
But each and every trial was approved at the throne of grace.
The valley at times is deep- the road may be stony and rough,
But God's grace is still sufficient, even when times are tough.
How we handle the trials in life depends upon our faith-
And just how much we trust Him, and claim unfailing grace.
We can choose to carry our burdens —to handle them on our own,
But our Father waits to claim them —He says we are not alone.
If you look behind the clouds in the trial - longing to be healed-
You are in the middle of a miracle, just waiting to be revealed.
There is victory in each valley-through each and every trial-
Let the Lord have full control —and He will return your smile.
Worry slanders every promise the Heavenly Father has made—
Our lives are what He wants them to be —
if at His feet they're laid.

Given to me by the Lord with victory in the valley
Jerry L Schock
1/20/2013

Phil 4:6 "Be careful for nothing; but in every thing by prayer and supplication with thanksgiving let your requests be made known unto God.."

We Cannot Carry the Burden

We cannot carry the burden Lord – it is too hard we plea -
Hold on my precious child–this care was meant for me.
The burdens of those we love are sent from God above,
For us to carry together – in splendid Christian love.
A burden is so hard to bear when we try to carry it alone,
And so the Father sent the Son –and angels from the throne.
They come through a smile, a hug or even a special touch -
But all are sent from Heaven –to those we love so much.

Given to me by the Lord

Galatians 6:2
By Jerry L Schock 8/24/02

What if We Knew?

Sometimes our Heavenly Father, allows the shadows to come,
We may even find we're fearing the thing to us that's unknown.
We often sit and wonder – so many questions in our mind,
But things that are hidden from us –are because He is so kind.
What if we knew the future? What of the trials we'll face?
How would we ever learn to rest on God's unchanging grace?
We'd be trying to change things-to make them go our way,
And surely as Heaven awaits us – we would go astray.
So let's try not to question –our Father in Heaven above,
Let's try to learn to trust Him – resting in His love.
Leave unanswered questions, to the One who knows best,
Finding peace and comfort, leaning only on His breast.

3-10-00
Jerry L. Schock

When God Made the Father

When God made the father- He had a special plan
He wanted one who would love and lend a helping hand.
Someone who would be a guide on the path of life-
Who would care for his children and also love his wife.
He planted deep within him a yearning for the Lord,
And gave him a desire to read God's Holy Word.
Today is set aside so we may give special honor-
To the gift God gave us that we call our father
Whether here with us or gone to Heaven above
Today we want to honor each of them with love.

Happy Fathers Day
From the Adult Auditorium
Sunday School Class

Miss Jerry Lee Schock

When We Can Do No More

At times Lord the burden is so great we cannot even pray-
We long within our hearts to see the sunshine's ray.
We ask You move the clouds and take away the rain-
Take us from the valley and make us whole again.
Then suddenly without warning, You move the clouds away-
You show us by Your loving Hand-the light of a brand new day-
You send a special unexpected blessing from Heaven up above-
And shower us in that blessing with care and peace and love.
If only we could learn to let go of the heavy load-
And trust in your provision as we walk a rocky road-
By letting go and letting God we learn the lesson anew-
That the only thing that will never
change, is our love from You.
So the next time there is a valley that seems too deep & wide-
Remind us precious Lord –that You are by our side.
The one thing you ask is faith and our full trust in You-
Help us remember Lord-Your promises are true.

Given to me by the Lord for my sister, Linda
Jerry L Schock
4/20/13

Heb. 13:15 for he hath said,
I will never leave thee, nor forsake thee.

When We Cannot Understand

Dear Lord I often wonder, just why You let it be,
When those we love are suffering- and reasons we cannot see.
But deep within this heart I know-Your love will never change,
And yet when we see suffering – it makes us feel so strange.
We see Your hand of mercy and protection through it all-
You've never failed to be there, anytime we call..
You take the circumstances that seem impossible to bear-
Turn around and use them to show how much You care.
You provide through times of trial - when the way we cannot see-
And raise us up on mountains when our spirits want to flee.
You calm the storms around us and then You dry the tears-
You surround us with Your peace and take away our fears.
So Lord I pray You help us-as we wait upon Your Will-
Help our faith to grow in trials- as You whisper 'peace, be still".

Jerry L Schock

When You Will Not Let Me Rest

Father here I am again in the early hours of the morn,
Another precious one in my prayers, who is weary and worn.
I cannot get her off my mind as for her intercession I make;
And as I pray, if it be Your will, from her the burden take.
Oh how my heart aches for her Lord, I can almost feel the pain,
But through my life I've learned, that is often how we gain.
Father I don't know what the need is, but I do know that it's there,
And I am asking you to meet that need, wrap her in Your care.
Hold her close and let her feel Your precious Presence ever near,
As You comfort now this sister, that I've learned to hold so dear.
I know there are times You will ask us to walk in a valley so deep,
But You will never leave us alone, Your promises You keep.
Sometimes when the storm around us rages-
When we see nothing but rain,
That's when You draw us closer to the blessed rock of ages-
And peace surrounds us once again.

By JERRY L SCHOCK

Inspired by a sermon preached 06/08/10 at the
National GPA Camp meeting by Dr. Tolbert Moore

Who Is the Gospel For

Where should we go, whom should we tell the gospel story to?
Into all the world the preacher said, God's instruction to you.
Go in His authority –taking the gospel to every man.
Whosoever will may come-that is the Master's plan.

No man should ever die in sin, because we failed to care
Or because we made the decision with whom we are to share-
God will open to us every door as we journey on the way,
If we go only in His power, and take the time to pray.

We're limited by human power, following the Lord's command
But His authority or power has no limit anywhere in the land.
He promises to be with us everywhere –not sending us on our own,
He says "… lo, I am with you always…" you will not go alone.

Matt 28:16-20 "…All power is given unto me in heaven and in earth."

Given to me by the Lord
06/12/10
Jerry L Schock

Yet Another Valley

*There is yet another valley and we do not understand,
But in our hearts there is no doubt, all is in Your hand.
Life has taught us many things as each trial we go through,
But always we have found, we can depend on You.
My heart is aching Lord as I watch them in this trial,
And with each step they take, I see behind their smile.
Fear of just not knowing what it is that lies ahead,
Can sometimes break our hearts and make us feel the dread.
One thing of this I'm sure, the road was traveled before,
You have gone ahead and prepared the way once more.
The steps that are in the valley may be rocky it is true,
But nothing we face in this life is ever a surprise to you.
So hold them very close to You as they face another trail,
And surround them with a peace that will truly bring a smile.
Place Your arms about them –remind them how much You care –
Bear up their precious husbands; let them know You're there.
Send angels to heal and protect and intercessors to pray-
'Till the sun shines 'round them again,
and they see the light of day.*

Given to me by the Lord for Martha and Barbara
Jerry L Schock
8/5/12

My Journey Thus Far

God is allowing my story to be told in print with this book.

When Mom and Dad were first divorced my Grandma Herman told Mom she could not raise us alone. Grandma told her to put us in the children's home and Mom said no. She said she would raise us no matter how many jobs it took She always said she was not raising us alone-God was watching over us.

For a while we stayed with Grandma and Grandpa Herman. Since I was the first granddaughter and born on Grandpa's 77th birthday-he favored me. Every Saturday morning, he and I would walk down the back alley the several blocks to Andy's Market. I loved garlic bologna and he would buy me a ring of garlic bologna and get his block of limburger cheese. Mom loved that too, but I could never even taste it. On the way home we would stop at the Texaco station and he would get me a chocolate bar. We would sit at that big kitchen table he had built-being a carpenter by trade- and he would get the saltine crackers, cut up the bologna for me and then start on his cheese. Grandpa loved the Cincinnati Red's baseball team and we would watch it on TV-him in his easy chair-me at his feet and his parakeet, Petey on his head. Good memories.

We later moved to Parkside homes and on Sunday-Mom would put my youngest brother in the stroller-Stan behind him -and I would hold onto the bar. We would walk across the grassy area to the Lutheran church for Sunday School. As we got older, we moved closer to downtown Dayton and the 3 of us would walk to the City Mission for Sunday School. Hobart and Thelma Roark handled services there. They owned a fur shop and furniture store in Laura, OH., and went to Westwood Baptist Church.

Thelma took an interest in me and Mom would let her take me on Friday and stay with them until after church Sunday. Saturday we would go for a walk and then back home to eat and clean up. Then to the furniture store where she played the piano or organ and I would sing. The manager, Dick Foreman taught me how to greet customers. My first exposure to what became my career, the furniture business.

Saved at age 13 at the Westwood Baptist Church in Dayton, I wanted to tell everyone how to get saved. Mom worked at the YMCA as a cashier in the cafeteria and had exchange students from the Dominican Republic. I invited Ramon Diaz to church. Taking my first visitor to church felt good, UNTIL we got into the church. 63 years later I STILL remember the cold feeling going down that aisle -it was as if someone poured a tray of ice over the entire church! All because his skin was darker. After quite a while my Sunday School teacher took me home and told Mom to pull me out of the church because I was being persecuted as I thought everyone should be treated the same My heart was broken but I determined to become a Missionary nurse and go to Africa so I could spread the gospel.

We were raised to believe the color of one's skin had nothing to do with anything-we did not know the word prejudice. We all went to school together from grade school through high and wondered what the big deal was when in the early 60's they said the schools in Dayton were to be integrated-we had always been together. My best friend all the way through school was Virginia Glanton, a black girl. Mom said you could cut anyone and we ALL would bleed red. Mom had a Dayton Daily Newspaper branch as one of her 3 jobs and we had a bowling team and a baseball team. One Saturday morning Mom took us bowling for the news branch to a bowling alley on Brown Street. One of our carriers was Calvin Jones -a black boy-and the manager of the bowling alley pointed at him when we went in to get our shoes and said "he can't bowl here". But Mom said, "if he can't bowl then none of us will and NO ONE from the Dayton Daily News will ever bowl here again". Needless to say we ALL bowled- and integrated that bowling alley then and there!

Even though I found another church it was not the same –I graduated from Stivers High School high school in 1961 -10th in a graduating class of

161. Two highlights in school were the lead part I had in "Oklahoma" and the Bible Club teacher asking me to speak. When asked what I wanted to speak on I said faith and she wrote the word acrostically and it said Forsaking All I Take Him. I have never forgotten it.

I started nurses training at Miami Valley Hospital and during my first year-allowed a man 8 years older than myself to take advantage of me. Thank God He forgives our failures when we confess and ask. Although Doug did all he could to make me lose my baby he failed. He got married the day before we were to be. Unmarried and pregnant-I turned to my best friend-Mom. When I called and told her she just said, "you better pack your clothes and come home".

Bobby Joe was born November 14, 1962. We lived at home for a few years and then moved to West Carrollton, OH. with a friend who had a son the same age as Bobby. We eventually got our own apartment and I bought a car. When the job at Penker Construction ended, I went around the corner to Roberts furniture to apply for a job-where they sold everything for the home. Howard Smith gave me a customer to see what I could do and when I sold a pair of lamps, hired me-saying if I could sell accessories, I could sell anything. Worked there until the owner bankrupted the company and moved back to Kentucky. In 1971, Ken Fletcher, Howard Smith and Don Wright bought the bankrupt stock. Ken called and asked if I wanted to come back to work-said Smitty told him if they were to succeed -they needed me. Of course, I did!! We could not afford a new sign so changed the name from ROBERTS to ROBERDS -switching the **T to a D** and thus Roberds Furniture was started.

Over time we had a total of 28 stores/distribution centers in 4 states and except for two in GA -I was instrumental in opening all of them as corporate coordinator. I was in FL opening 2 new stores when Bobby Joe was killed in a motorcycle wreck May 21, 1986. Neighbors said the police had been to the house God let me buy in 1974, several times to let me know and when they could not reach me, called my brother Jerry-whom they knew was a Deputy for Montgomery County. and he called my boss. Ken Fletcher did not know the Lord as far as I know but I prayed daily for him. He did not want me to talk about the Lord at work. Still He had my preacher come to the store to call me in FL to let me know. God had already arranged things as He always does.

Mom had retired at 65 on May 10th -her birthday- from the YMCA and Ken asked her at Bobby's funeral if she was going to move into my house- telling her I did not need it as I would be traveling. She said yes and Jerry moved her in June 1st. Mom lived there until she went home to be with the Lord July 19, 2011. After my move to GA the rent and payments was too much but both of my brothers offered to split the house payment and it was done 3 ways so Mom could stay where she was happiest.

I had asked to move to FLORIDA in 1987 and continued to open stores between GA and FL and OH. June of 1992, Ken called telling me we had stores in trouble in GA and he needed me to move there since I was the only one who could fix it. Serving and settled in my church-I told Ken I had to pray about it-I heard a gasp on the other end of the phone but that is all I can do when a decision is needed. He asked how long it would take to get an answer and I was confident God would let me know by Monday and told him so. He told me it would mean a $24000.00 salary and I had to be sure God was in the move not me. I prayed all weekend and only asked 2 things of the Lord so I would KNOW it was Him, not me. I said Lord please do not ever let me drive on 85 and not one dime will come out of my pocket to make the move (The company paid no expenses ahead of time). Monday, I called and asked the questions-they would get my apartment -pay first month's rent and deposit and all utility deposits would be made-close to the store. And, they would give me a check for the $3000.00 moving expense ahead of time. So, feeling confident it WAS God in charge-I said I would go-and he wanted me there in 3 weeks. I made some calls from the Shepherd's guide to see what churches were near Norcross and the first call was Galilean Baptist and 27 years later I am still there-God always knows where we belong, and I have never had to drive 85 or 285 to get to work. July 14, 1992, I moved my letter to Galilean and the 2nd week Ollie and Linda "adopted" me into their family. Linda's favorite saying is we are all kin under the skin. Even though they never met Mom they loved her and she loved them.

With the move to GA I uncovered over $450,000.00 that had been stolen from the company and we moved the thieves out. Taking over inventory control helped and by December we had 21 people behind bars for theft.

We continued to open stores in all markets as I traveled from GA to FL to OH. In 1996 we opened Roberds Grand in Cincinnati, OH. -a megastore- nearly 6 acres, larger than Riverfront Stadium.

I lived in the apartment until 1997 and signed the papers on my birthday to buy a condo-after the apartment owners wanted to raise the rent over $100.00 per month. I saw an ad for a realtor on TV and called Sherrell to ask where she went to church. She told me and asked why? I explained God knew where I needed to be but if she did not know Him she could not listen to Him. It was clear God let me know I could spend $60,000.00 for a condo and she told me I would never find one for that. I explained she could not nor could I- but He knew where it was and 22 years later, I am still here (price was $59,900.00).

After opening a Distribution Center in GA-we moved our appliance and furniture Customer Service teams there. Every morning some of us would meet in my office and pray for one another and the business. June of 1999, our CFO from corporate called and Bob said he understood I was having prayer meetings in my office. I said yes, he told me he loved me and I know he did-but he could not allow me to continue, etc. I told him if he took God's hand off the business, we would lose it and he said he could not help it-Dec. that year the company filed a Chapter 13. By June, 2000, the liquidators were scheduled in and not wishing to watch nearly 30 years of my life's work torn apart-I took my 3 weeks vacation and resigned, without prospects. I went home and remember laying my keys on the coffee table and telling the Lord I NEVER wanted to be in the furniture business again. Three weeks later I was working for a computer company in Covington where one of my road techs had gone. By October it became evident there was something else awaiting and after praying about it I resigned.

Nov. 2000, a call came from one of young men that had been at Roberds and was now at the then Plan It Oak-asking if I was working-he said we have had the rest now want the best-they needed someone to run Customer Service. Nov 7th when I went to work there my entire work life changed for the better!! Thanksgiving meant the company provided meat and we all brought side dishes in for the meal. As we gathered in the break room at the warehouse-Mike Hall -the owner-asked if I would pray!! I was sure I had died and gone to Heaven!! In the nearly 18 years I worked -Mike and Tim encouraged me to pray-spread the gospel and lead our folks to the Lord. When Mike handed me my ring for 10 years of service-he kindly said, "If we have a spiritual leader-it is Jerry". I am truly blessed. Several young people will be in Heaven because of the freedom they gave me. I have thanked God many times for NOT listening to me. I finally retired Sept 2018.

One of most wonderful blessings going to work for Mike has been my "adopted" granddaughter Gladys Everson -she calls me Nana. Most of the kids at work still call me that. I am ever so grateful we did not learn prejudice growing up or I would have missed this sweet girl and the sisters God gave me at church.

All the wonderful names I have been called down thru the years and the sweet things that have been said are flooding my mind. I remember Mom saying if you have something to do-do it today-tomorrow may not come. So here goes-As I have told everyone who was so complimentary all my life -ALL the glory belongs to the Lord-not me. I am rotten to the core. I remember Mom telling me when God made me-He threw the mold away because the world could not stand 2 of me. Well, I believe it. I have a big mouth. Bona Griffieth told me I was one of the things they told her to watch out for when she was hired at Roberds, because I would try to get her saved. They did not know she was a Christian and the Lord worked it out she flew home with me when Bobby Joe died. HEY I LOVE that reputation and gladly claim it still today. even on the phone God gives me that boldness.

Bona sent me a sweet note after I returned to thank me for showing her faith. Then I got a wonderful letter from Travis Hudson, my Pastor at Moraine Heights Baptist Church. He said after nearly 40 years of preaching-he had never seen faith-until he saw me at Bobby's funeral and thanked me. Clemmon Chappell-one of our preachers said I was his Epaphroditus -Rick Glass another GPA preacher-called me our GPA prayer warrior-Bro Dennis Harkins thanked me for being his and his wife's Barnabus. Bro Jim Moore called me a prophetess one morning as he asked I pray for his eye-and the Bro Tolbert Moore at his 90th birthday —was sitting next to a preacher across from me and said he always watched me during the service and if he saw my hand go up he knew the service was okay -if not he wondered what was wrong-because I knew how to get hold of the Holy Spirit. I love you ALL for those kind words.

ALL the glory belongs to Jesus!! I am just so grateful to KNOW why I am on this earth and He enables me to fulfill my commission. He put me here to be a good prayer warrior and an encourager (and He is continually adding to the 3 ecxel workbooks of names that are called in prayer every Saturday) and of course there is a daily list. Any good you see in me is the LORD. Thanks to ALL of you who allow me to pray for you and encourage you when you are in need. As long as God gives me breath I will continue on this journey of intercessory prayer and encouragement.

Why I Wrote A Book

Many ask why I wrote these books. First, God put me here to be a good prayer warrior and encourager. Poems provide encouragement. The journey to publishing, with God's leading, has not been a hard one. Mother told me from my teenage years there was an angel sitting on my shoulder and she had watched that angel work things out for me that would never work out for anyone else. Seeking God's will made each step much easier. Having been blessed for more than 60 plus years to write poetry for those the Lord sent my way who were hurting, the answer to the question is simply For God's Glory. One of the first people to encourage me to publish was my sister-in-law, Pat and I said "when God's ready I will." In January 2018 I began to seek God's leading on how to start the process. Thus my journey to become an author began. I started through my filing cabinet as much of the poetry had been printed, creating the documents to submit to the publisher. Since publishing April 14, 2018, royalties have gone to the GPA at Galilean Baptist Church In Lawrenceville, GA to support missionaries.

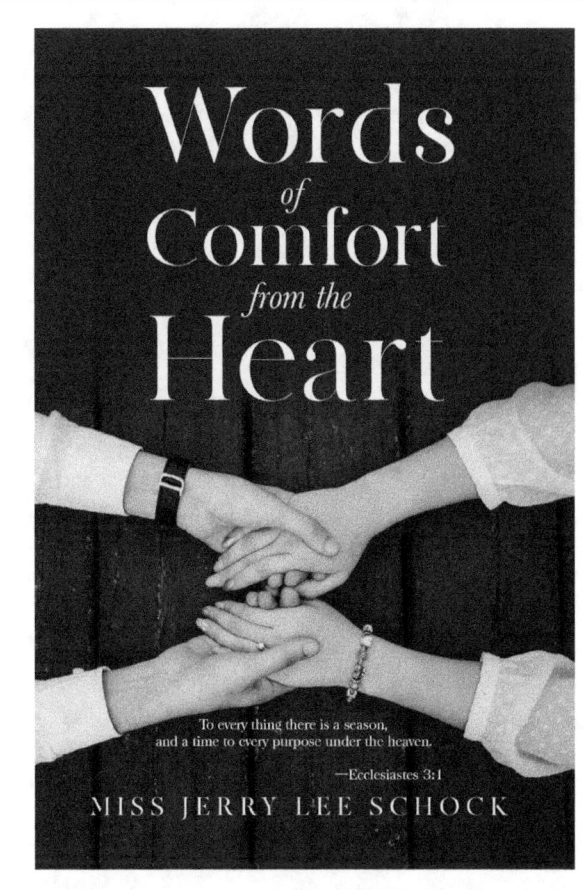

The Gospel Preachers Association
at **Galilean Baptist Church**

1390 Monfort Rd,
Lawrenceville, GA 30046, United States
770 995 7045